I Wait IN HIM

31 Quiet Moments with God

Leonie H. Mattison, Ed.D., MBA

Copyright © 2020 by Leonie H. Mattison, Ed.D.

All rights reserved. No part of this publication may be reproduced, stored in a retrieval system, or transmitted in any form or by any means—including photocopying, recording, or other electronic or mechanical methods—without the prior written permission of the publisher. The only exception is brief quotations in printed reviews.

Printed in the United States of America
First Printing, 2020

ISBN 978-1-7332966-8-7

The Thread, LLC
www.leoniemattison.com

All Scripture quotations, unless otherwise indicated, are taken from the Holy Bible, New Living Translation, copyright ©1996, 2004, 2015 by Tyndale House Foundation. Used by permission of Tyndale House Publishers, Inc., Carol Stream, Illinois 60188. All rights reserved.

Scripture quotations marked EASY are taken from the Easy English Bible Copyright © Mission Assist 2019 – Charitable Incorporated Organization 1162807. Used by permission. All rights reserved.

Scripture quotations marked MSG are taken from THE MESSAGE, copyright © 1993, 2002, 2018 by Eugene H. Peterson. Used by permission of NavPress. All rights reserved. Represented by Tyndale House Publishers, Inc.

Scripture quotations marked TLB are taken from The Living Bible copyright © 1971. Used by permission of Tyndale House Publishers, a Division of Tyndale House Ministries, Carol Stream, Illinois 60188. All rights reserved.

Scripture quotations marked CSB are been taken from the Christian Standard Bible®, Copyright © 2017 by Holman Bible Publishers. Used by permission. Christian Standard Bible, and CSB® are federally registered trademarks of Holman Bible Publishers.

Scripture quotations marker KJV are taken from the King James Version. Public domain.

Scripture quotations marked TPT are from The Passion Translation®. Copyright © 2017, 2018 by Passion & Fire Ministries, Inc. Used by permission. All rights reserved. ThePassionTranslation.com.

Scripture quotations marked GNT are from the Good News Translation in Today's English Version- Second Edition Copyright © 1992 by American Bible Society. Used by Permission.

Photos by https://unsplash.com

To

_____

From

_____

Date

_____

Contents

Welcome viii

Day 1   Wait in the Lord 2

Day 2   Rise Up and Praise Him 4

Day 3   Rid Yourself of Distractions 6

Day 4   Cast Your Cares on Him 8

Day 5   His Unfailing Love 10

Day 6   His Faithful Forgiveness 12

Day 7   Have Faith in the Process 14

Day 8   Praying with Faith 16

Day 9   Hear His Words 18

Day 10   Great Expectation 20

Day 11   Trust in the Waiting 22

Day 12   Trust in His Knowledge 24

Day 13   Trust in His Word 26

Day 14   Trust in His Rebuilding 28

Day 15	Trust in the Gospel	30
Day 16	Trust in His Planting	32
Day 17	Trust in the Pruning	34
Day 18	Trust in His Connection	36
Day 19	Trust in His Strength	38
Day 20	Trust in His Glory	40
Day 21	Restore My Redemption	42
Day 22	A Full Restoration	44
Day 23	Clinging to His Word	46
Day 24	Restore My Hope	48
Day 25	A Strong Anchor	50
Day 26	Restoration in the Silence	52
Day 27	Wait with Action	54
Day 28	Wait with Praise	56
Day 29	Restore My Joy	58
Day 30	Restore My Purpose	60
Day 31	Wait with Preparation	62

Welcome

"Whenever my busy thoughts were out of control, the soothing comfort of your presence calmed me down and overwhelmed me with delight." Psalms 94:19 TPT

How did we get here? It's been three months since the coronavirus forced the world into total isolation. We were made to shelter at home and wait. We could not leave our homes because outside the door breathed death. To stay safe, we had to practice physical distancing by staying in seclusion in our homes and waiting. But the longer I waited, the more unbearable it felt. There were days when I found myself wrestling, reasoning, bargaining, and pleading with God to manifest healing.

Little did I know that God often answers our prayers in ways we never expect.

One morning during my devotion time, I experienced a visitation from the Holy Spirit. When I invited Him in, He whispered, "Leonie, what if

while waiting *on* the Lord, you waited *in* the Lord?" Immediately I was reminded of Luke 12:24: "Take the carefree birds as your example. Do you ever see them worry? They don't grow their own food or put it in a storehouse for later. Yet God takes care of every one of them, feeding each of them from his love and goodness. Isn't your life more precious to God than a bird? Be carefree in the care of God!" (TPT)

In that moment I realized that the word *in* indicates inclusion within something abstract. Here's the truth: *Every breakthrough, every miracle, every promise fulfilled, every battle won, every strength gained, every growth achieved, every miracle received, every healing experienced—requires a wait.*

Why is waiting so difficult? Our perceptions are not always God's will. God rarely does things according to our time frame. He is strategic, intentional, and precise. Often, the Lord uses waiting as a development tool that forces us to cease our striving and rest in Him. It is while waiting that He changes our heart and brings us to His presence, purpose, and perfect will. Waiting can make us feel lonely, or think that God is uncaring or mad at us, because during the waiting season we are being set apart to be alone with God. But here's the thing: God is silent when He's at work!

Wait in Him, a 31-day devotion will walk you through how to wait *in* the Lord while you wait on Him. My prayer is that by the end of this devotional, you will find yourself more connected to God and His Word. I pray you will find joy, renew your faith, and discover hope, maybe for the first time.

In my experience, waiting takes courage. During this season, I have made a point to not get so caught up in when God will end the waiting period that I end up forfeiting what He's doing in me. The only thing harder than waiting on God is wishing that you had. So, "Be still in the presence of the Lord, and wait patiently for him to act" (Psalm 37:7). "Wait for the Lord; be strong, and let your heart be courageous. Wait for the Lord" (Psalms 27:14 CSB).

Oh, child of God, wait *in* the Lord and delight in your mission today!

What waiting *in* God taught me is captured in this note to you.

Sometimes God uses waiting in Him to:

Arrange our circumstances
Build our character
Consecrate our hearts
Do a new thing in our life
Empower us for the journey
Focus us on His Word
Guide us in unexpected ways
Help us hear His instructions
Increase our faith
Join us to Himself
Keep us steadfast and unmovable
Launch us into our destiny
Move us into His purpose.
Nourish and nurture our hearts
Open the eyes of our understanding
Prepare and equip us for where He's taking us
Quiet our mind so we can focus on Him
Remove us from distraction
Slow us down
Teach us patience in our daily walk
Uncover who we are becoming in the next season
Visit with us on a one-to-one basis
Withdraw us to Himself
X-ray our hearts
Yield to His will

Waiting is not a stop but a pause!

Day 1

WAIT IN THE LORD

Be still in the presence of the LORD, *and wait patiently for him to act.*

Psalm 37:7

Wait for the Lord. What if that waiting feels long and hard? What if the waiting feels as though a prayer is going unanswered? God asks us to find our hope *in* Him and rest *in* Him. He asks us to wait *patiently* for Him.

That isn't easy. Many times our waiting is like how a toddler waits for their parent to get them something. If you've seen a toddler wait, you know it's not something they do patiently. They either get upset or lose focus and do something else. Like a toddler, we tend to busy ourselves until we're no longer focused on our Father or waiting patiently. This is a perfect picture of waiting *for* someone, but waiting *on* someone or something means to remain inactive or to continue on in expectation of something.

What if we change our thinking? What if while we're waiting *on* the Lord, we waited *in* the Lord. The word *in* indicates inclusion within something abstract. Maybe if we remain *in* Him, with Him, for Him, and allow ourselves to be found entirely in Him, we will find peace, comfort, and—ultimately—rest. SEE yourself wrapped in the Father's arms today and LISTEN to His words as He tells you of His faithfulness.

Think About This

What has your journey with the Lord been like so far? Do you tend to wait *in* Him or simply wait on Him to do something for you? Why do you think this is?

> *Lord, sometimes I tend to just wait on You to do something, and in my waiting I become impatient. Help me to trust in Your faithfulness and wait* in *You, O Lord.*

Day 2

RISE UP AND PRAISE HIM

> *I look up to the mountains—*
> *   does my help come from there?*
> *My help comes from the LORD,*
> *   who made heaven and earth!*
>
> Psalm 121:1–2

Wait, oh, sweet child of God. In the middle of your waiting, wait patiently in the Lord.

Waiting *in* the Lord implies taking action. Pursue Him while you are waiting. He is near and can be found. We tend to look in so many other places for our help, such as our friends, our families, and self-help books, just to name a few. While these avenues can provide some temporary help, they cannot provide the eternal help and guidance we need.

Only when you LOOK up to the hills and SEE the Lord and His throne, can you begin to take action. You can SING His praises and READ His

Word for strength. He is faithful and will move in the midst of your waiting if you allow Him to.

Think About This

How can you find your hope in the Lord while you're waiting *in* Him? What actions do you need to take today to really listen to His voice through His Word?

> *Lord, help me rise up and take action while I'm waiting in You. Whether that's reading Your Word and looking for help and answers, or singing Your praises in worship. May I find You, my Help.*

Day 3

RID YOURSELF OF DISTRACTIONS

And now, dear brothers and sisters, one final thing. Fix your thoughts on what is true, and honorable, and right, and pure, and lovely, and admirable. Think about things that are excellent and worthy of praise.

Philippians 4:8

While waiting, other things may try to take priority. These things tend to cloud our view and become distractions from our waiting. In Philippians, Paul tells us to fix our eyes on the things of God instead of earthly things—things that are true, honorable, right, pure, lovely, and admirable. Those things are excellent and worthy of praise. Waiting *in* Him requires a mind shift, and part of that shift is focusing on godly things that will build us up and encourage us instead of tearing us down.

READ the words in Philippians 4:8, and BREATHE in the presence of God. THINK about His goodness, His righteousness, and His faithfulness. Let His Words envelop you.

Think About This

How do these attributes of God compare to the characteristics of man? What makes God so worthy of our praise?

> *Lord, I will focus on who You are and how You are worthy of my praise. Help me lift my voice in good times and bad. Thank You for Your faithfulness.*

Day 4

CAST YOUR CARES ON HIM

Give all your worries and cares to God, for he cares about you.

1 Peter 5:7

Throughout this time of waiting, you may experience many different emotions. Sometimes you may feel His joy in your heart as you take comfort in His promises. Other times you may feel anxiety as you wonder about the days to come. You may even feel sorrow for relationships lost or things in your past. Know that through it all, He is faithful. He will replace your difficult emotions with the peace you need to make it through.

LEAN in—all in—as you navigate these uncomfortable emotions. Cast your cares on Him. He is big enough to take all your worries and faithful enough to see you through. HEAR His Words of faithfulness as you READ this great promise.

Think About This

What are some of the fears you have about waiting *in* the Lord? How can you cast your cares on Him and leave them there?

> *Lord, You are good and faithful. You promise us that if we give You our worries and fears, You will take them on. You will see me through. Thank You for how You carry my burdens.*

Day 5

His Unfailing Love

For his unfailing love for us is powerful; the LORD's faithfulness endures forever.

Psalm 117:2

Have faith in the love of the Lord. Allow His love to wrap you up while you're waiting *in* Him. His passion is unfailing and unending. The greatest love that man can give is still temporary at best. It fails from time to time and may end if someone feels wronged. Only when we rely on His love can we love like He does. His passion is powerful and can help us in our time of trial when we need patience, wisdom, understanding, and comfort. It can heal over time. When we rely on His mighty love, we experience His faithfulness. His faithfulness endures forever. In short, His love is faithful and never fails.

FEEL the presence of God and His unfailing love in your life. LEAN into the Lord and FEEL His love wrap itself around you. Allow yourself to give in to this great love.

Think About This

How do you feel His love? Who can you show Christ's love to today?

Lord, I wrap myself up in Your love today. May I feel Your faithfulness and know that the only kind of unconditional love I will ever find is in Your mighty love. Thank You for showing me how to love others.

Day 6

His Faithful Forgiveness

If we confess our sins, [God] is faithful and just to forgive us our sins and to cleanse us from all unrighteousness.

1 John 1:9

The Lord is faithful to forgive our sins. There is no sin that He can't forgive. His forgiveness is complete. His mercy is forever. When man forgives, this forgiveness often comes with conditions: "I'll only forgive you if…" Sometimes it's even taken back or the person gives a reminder of the sin over and over again. But God is faithful in His forgiveness. He will forgive and throw the crime and the reminders of sin as far as the east is from the west. This verse tells us that all we have to do is confess our sins. He is faithful and just to forgive us, *and* He will cleanse us from all wrongdoing. He will give us a new start.

Have faith in His forgiveness. LISTEN to Him tell you, "Your sins are forgiven, child." SEE Him wipe your slate clean.

Think About This

What does our forgiveness look like when someone wrongs us? What does God's mercy look like?

> *Lord, forgive me for all of my shortcomings and wrongdoings. Remind me of how faithful You are. Remind me of how You don't bring up my past like others do. Help me to see Your faithfulness in my story.*

Day 7

Have Faith in the Process

Some of you were once like that. But you were cleansed; you were made holy; you were made right with God by calling on the name of the Lord Jesus Christ and by the Spirit of our God.

1 Corinthians 6:11

Once we accept Christ's great gift of salvation and He washes us clean, He begins a process of sanctification in our lives. To sanctify means to set apart, purify, or make holy. This is a process that starts at the moment of salvation and is fulfilled when we get to heaven. It is a constant process, much like water running in a stream. If the water is moving toward something, it naturally becomes purified; however, the minute it stands still, the water becomes muddy and messy. During this time of waiting in the Lord, it is essential to move, or be active, in our spiritual lives. When we are busy, we continuously allow God to transform our lives and purify us. Have faith in this sanctification process, trusting that God will be faithful to complete your salvation.

WRITE down the many ways that Christ has transformed your life, so you can SEE the sanctification process. BREATHE in His grace and forgiveness, and THANK Him for doing a work in your life.

Think About This

What was your life like before Christ's transformation? How did your life change after salvation?

> *Lord, thank You for rescuing me from a life of sin. I know that You are doing a work in me, and I have faith that You will continue to transform my life. Help me trust in Your faithfulness.*

Day 8

PRAYING WITH FAITH

I tell you, you can pray for anything, and if you believe that you've received it, it will be yours.

Mark 11:24

One way to be active in our waiting is to pray. We tend to choose prayer as a last resort, thinking that prayer is passive, but it's actually an action. When we pray, we're calling on the power of God to act in our life or someone else's. James 5:16 says the earnest prayer of a righteous man has high potential and produces beautiful results. Your prayers are not only powerful but also practical! So instead of worship being your last resort, make it the first action you take while you are waiting *in* the Lord.

Prayer is communication with God. We feel close to those in our lives when we're in contact with them, so when you communicate with God, you are close to Him. Waiting in the Lord requires you to maintain close communication with God through prayer! Open the Bible, READ His promises, and FEEL the power of prayer as you SPEAK those prayers to God your Father.

Think About This

How do you see prayer? Is it formal, or is it a casual conversation? How can you pray as though you are speaking to God?

> *Lord, help me be more active in my waiting by communicating with You through prayer. Give me confidence as I speak words of truth over my life and others' lives.*

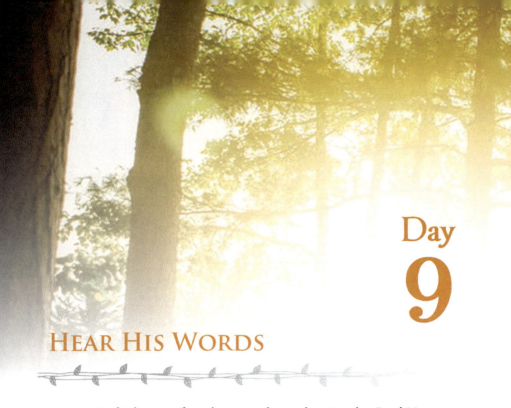

Day 9

HEAR HIS WORDS

So faith comes from hearing, that is, hearing the Good News about Christ.

Romans 10:17

Faith comes from hearing. When we hear someone say they will do something for us, we typically have confidence that they will see it through and fulfill their promise (unless they have shown us otherwise in the past). The same is true when we read God's Word. The Bible offers words that bring peace and comfort, provide guidance in our lives, and ultimately give us life. When we read His Word, we find joy, hope, and *faith*. This is another way we can be active while waiting *in* the Lord.

To really HEAR the words of Christ, you must open the Bible, SEE His words, and then READ them aloud so you HEAR His promises. When you do this, your faith will be strengthened.

Think About This

What promises in God's Word give you hope and strengthen your faith? How does reading the Bible help you stay active in your relationship with God and support you while you wait *in* Him?

> *Lord, help me be active in my relationship with You by reading Your Word and relying on Your promises. Strengthen my faith through reading and hearing your words.*

Day 10

GREAT EXPECTATION

Be on guard. Stand firm in the faith. Be courageous. Be strong.

1 Corinthians 16:13

You probably know what waiting on someone is like. It can feel like an eternity! We can become impatient and even get distracted while we wait. However, by changing our focus from waiting *on* the Lord to waiting *in* the Lord, we take action while remaining in close communion with Him.

This verse tells us to be watchful. Always be on guard, making sure that nothing distracts you from focusing on the Lord. Stand firm in the faith. Be sure you have a firm foundation rooted in action. We stand firm by being active in prayer and our study of the Word. Be courageous and be healthy. Have courage while you wait, knowing and trusting that God is always moving and working on your behalf. Have faith, and expect Him to do great things. Romans 8:28 tells us that He causes everything to work for good for those who love Him. This doesn't mean life will always be easy, but it promises that we have a God who loves us and cares for us. So wait *in* Him because it is the best place to be!

LEAN into the Lord to find your hope and experience the good He has for you. SEE yourself in close communion with the Father as a child on the lap of a beloved parent. FEEL His presence in your life.

Think About This

In what ways can you be courageous while you wait in the Lord?

> *Lord, You are faithful to me. You have done so many things in my life to show me Your faithfulness. Fill me with Your presence every day, so I may be able to guard my heart, stand in faith, and be courageous and strong. You are so good to me.*

Day 11

TRUST IN THE WAITING

Those who know your name trust in you, for you, O LORD, do not abandon those who search for you.

Psalm 9:10

What a beautiful declaration of waiting in the Lord. When we put our trust in the Lord, He does not abandon us. Throughout trials and tribulations, if we continue to place our hope in Him, He will sustain us.

The story of Joseph begins in Genesis 37. Joseph was the beloved son of Jacob; however, he was sold into slavery by his brothers because of their untamed jealousy, and eventually sold again. He remained faithful, and the Lord did not abandon him through his trials. The Lord continued to find favor with him. Joseph became a powerful man in Egypt and helped deliver the people from famine. The Lord kept His promise to Joseph and brought him together with his family once more.

Joseph was never forsaken by his Shepherd. He leaned in and waited *in* the Lord, never wasting a minute of his troubles. He testified of the Lord to those around him and used the gifts God gave him to speak words of truth through their dreams.

In these times of uncertainty and fear, do not waste the moments God is giving you. LEAN into Him. SPEAK these words aloud: "I trust You, Lord!" Then you will experience His promises just as Joseph did.

Think About This

What is God asking you to do during this time of quarantine? How can you trust Him more?

Thank you, Lord. I declare today that everyone will know that the living God is among us. Just as You were faithful in delivering the Israelites time and time again, You will be faithful in delivering Your people now from the COVID-19 pandemic. You will *deliver. Lord, help me trust in You like Joseph did throughout his many trials and tribulations.*

Day 12

TRUST IN HIS KNOWLEDGE

"I will confirm my covenant with you and your descendants after you, from generation to generation. This is the everlasting covenant: I will always be your God and the God of your descendants after you."

Genesis 17:7

No one understood God's promises and His faithfulness better than Abraham. Did he always trust in God's process? No. But he held tight to the hope that God would eventually make His people into a great nation. Abraham and Sarah had taken things into their own hands, so Abraham already had a son named Ishmael, but here God promised that through Sarah, Abraham would have a child who would bring forth His promises to him. Even so, Abraham struggled to trust the process God would use to fulfill His promise. He could see only what was in front of him, while God could see the entire picture. God had other plans and fulfilled His promise, despite anything Abraham or Sarah tried to do.

God has promises for us that we can take hold of as well. However, we need to make sure that while we're waiting *in* Him, we allow Him to work and trust that He will be the One to fulfill the promise to us. So in this season of waiting, LISTEN to His specific promises to you as you read the Word. SPEAK the words aloud as you trust in the Lord, and know that He can see the entire picture.

Think About This

What promises do you think God is trying to tell You that He will fulfill?

> *Lord, give me strength to forge forward despite low blows. I know that I don't know everything that's going on behind the scenes. Father, I know that Your Word will not return to You void. Help me keep Your word in my heart and mind, so that it renews, reshapes, revives, and sanctifies me. Help me focus my priorities on what matters to You. Sanctify my focus. I know You will supply all my needs. I know everyone will see Your glory, Lord, in all of these uncertain things.*

Day 13

Trust in His Word

All Scripture is inspired by God and is useful to teach us what is right and to make us realize what is wrong in our lives. It corrects us when we are wrong and teaches us to do what is right. God uses it to prepare and equip his people to do every good work.

2 Timothy 3:16–17

The Word of the Lord is powerful and active. What better tool to use than the Bible during these troubled times? In a battle, a soldier must be prepared and equipped; otherwise, he may find himself vulnerable. Just like a soldier should be ready for any situation, so should we as Christians. The Bible prepares us for battle against the Enemy, Satan, and equips us to defend ourselves against his ruthless attacks.

During the coronavirus pandemic, many people are finding themselves afraid and unprepared for the loneliness, depression, and anxiety that accompanies it. The Lord is the only One who knows how to handle this situation, but He is giving us the ability to stand against these things with the help of His Word. He will use this time to help us bear fruit, serve our communities and churches, and stay positive.

There is power in His Word, but if you don't spend quality time with Him and dig into the Word to experience His power, you will find ourselves defenseless. So LEAN into Him right now and open up His Word. BREATHE in His overwhelming presence and GRAB hold of the power He will give you.

Think About This

How can you be intentional about spending time in the Word and utilizing His power?

Father, release my need to know the details behind this virus. Give me a deep and compelling desire to wait in You, to identify You more, to bear more fruit, to be quieter before You, to satisfy Your will for my life, to serve the unchurched in new and different ways, and to stay steadfast and unmovable in Your love. Help me not to snuggle up to negativity and negative thinking, for You said in Your Word that You will not pour Your anointing into an unclean vessel. Jesus, deepen my desire to spend quality time with You. Thank You, Lord, for advancing the gospel during this season.

Day 14

TRUST IN HIS REBUILDING

"But if you return to me and obey my commands and live by them, then even if you are exiled to the ends of the earth, I will bring you back to the place I have chosen for my name to be honored."

Nehemiah 1:9

Nehemiah had a reasonably comfortable life enjoying the pleasures of Babylon. He had a prominent position in the king's court. However, after he heard from friends about the ruins of Jerusalem's walls and the vulnerability of his city, his heart was broken for the people, and he began to fast and pray. The city lay in ruins as a result of the people's sins, and they had spent the last seventy years paying for their crimes. Now they had begun to return to their broken city.

After fasting and praying, Nehemiah approached the king and asked to return to Jerusalem to help rebuild the walls and strengthen the town once again. Nehemiah sprang to action by fasting and praying while waiting *in* the Lord, and once he knew that was what God wanted him to do, he immediately began rebuilding.

No matter what your ruins look like, if you return to the Lord and live by His commands, He will rebuild you and make you more robust than before. He will uproot the mess that's been hindering the flow of the Holy Spirit in your body. He will rebuild you so you can bear the weight of this season.

Think About This

Is there something in your life that needs to be rebuilt? PRAY and SPEAK to your Father. ASK Him to restore your ruins.

> *Lord, help me to see that what You're doing in me, behind the scenes, beneath the surface and soil of my heart, is more important than what's happening to me. Nurture and feed my spirit as I dive and lean into Your Word. Keep my focus on You, Lord, and thank You for the fruit You're bearing in me.*

Day 15

Trust in the Gospel

Instead, you must worship Christ as Lord of your life. And if someone asks about your hope as a believer, always be ready to explain it. But do this gently and respectfully.

1 Peter 3:15–16

We, as a nation and world, need many things right now: jobs, health, a vaccine for the coronavirus, family, friends. However, the most significant thing this world needs is hope. Christians have the faith in Jesus Christ that people need.

The promise of the gospel saves us from depression, loneliness, and recklessness. God has given some of us time at home to think, fast, and pray for our world. For others, He has provided the chance to be His hands and feet to those around them. To many He has given a firsthand testimony of what He's doing on the frontlines. Whichever of these you identify with, we can be sure that God is doing a work in our lives. He is giving us opportunities to spread the gospel through our words on social media and our deeds in how we care for others. We are unable to physically share the gospel person to person, but mentally and spiritually we are equipped. This is our chance to be His hands and feet and put our worship into practice.

Use your time with Him, whether it's in the wee hours of the morning as you prepare for a day of serving others or whether you're spending your days with the Lord at home. LISTEN to worship music as you meditate about how you can spread the gospel to the hungry. LOOK for opportunities to share about what the Lord has done for you.

Think About This

How can you share the gospel with your neighbors, your friends, your family, and your coworkers during this unprecedented time?

> *Lord, show me what is important to You during this season of where I am feeling trapped inside what I don't yet know. Thank you, Lord! Jehovah-Shalom, things are taking an uncertain and negative turn for many of your children. Father, teach me to focus on the fruit—Your gospel—that's bearing much fruit. Yes, hallelujah. Lord, use me to focus on spreading the gospel. While we are waiting on daily instructions, Lord, lead us to worship. For it is in worship that You ready our hearts to receive what You're preparing for us.*

Day 16

TRUST IN HIS PLANTING

They are like trees planted along a riverbank,
*   with roots that reach deep into the water.*
Such trees are not bothered by the heat
*   or worried by long months of drought.*
Their leaves stay green,
*   and they never stop producing fruit.*

Jeremiah 17:8

We are in a season where we must focus on remaining planted in God. He gives us the roots, or the foundation, to stand tall through the turmoil and the waves of trials around us. We can become so deeply rooted in our faith and who He is that we can soak in the riches of His goodness and produce the fruit He desires. The trees in this Scripture are not scorched by the heat of the sun. They do not worry about drought. The beautiful thing about these trees is that they never stop producing fruit.

When we allow Him to plant us where He wants us and give us the nutrients we need through His Word, we will bear ripe fruit for the world to consume. We must remain where He has planted us by trusting that He is the One who knows our days and will handle them carefully. Even if we experience sorrows or troubles, He will never leave us and will hold us in His hands. SEE yourself being held by the Lord. BREATHE in His goodness.

Think About This

Where has God planted you? How can you bear fruit in this place?

Lord, You have so beautifully chosen the soil where I plant my feet. You handcrafted me and placed me in the ground to grow and blossom. May You water and care for me every day. Give me the nutrients I need through Your Word. I want to continue to grow into the person You have created me to be, so I can better serve You. I want to bear fruit that will bring others to You so they can find themselves in You and grow.

Day 17

TRUST IN THE PRUNING

*For I am like a tree whose roots reach the water,
whose branches are refreshed with the dew.*

Job 29:19

Part of growing in our faith and becoming closer in our relationship with God is allowing Him to prune our life. He can remove the things that hinder us, and lead us closer to Him. Sometimes that means a friendship or a modern-day idol like a material thing. While it can feel painful for a time, there is great reward in growing closer to the Lord. We will get to know Him more intimately while we wait *in* Him.

When you wait *in* him, He enlarges your faith, deepens your roots, and stretches you so you can gain more of His wisdom and character. Waiting in Him means allowing Him to take hold of your faith and lead you deeper and deeper until your heart is so grounded in Him that you can be confident in who you are and who He is in your life. As your roots reach the water, He will wash over you like a tidal wave, and you will feel His love refresh you. FEEL yourself moving toward the Lord.

Think About This

Is there anything or anyone keeping you from growing in the Lord? SPEAK to Him and ask Him to prune you so you can be refreshed in Him again.

> *Lord, help me focus on You while I wait in You. May my eyes focus only on You so I may grow closer to You. May my roots reach the water, Your living water. Refresh my life so I can bring glory to You. Lord, deepen my root system, teach me to be focused, and prune out of my life the things that would prevent me from bearing more fruit. Help me to LEAN into You, rely on You, and trust in You. Help me to know that You are working everything for my good.*

Day 18

Trust in His Connection

*They are like trees planted along the riverbank,
    bearing fruit each season.
Their leaves never wither,
    and they prosper in all they do.*

Psalm 1:3

Those who delight in the Lord will bear fruit that is ripe and ready for any who partake. Their leaves will never wither, and they will be successful—not in the way we would expect as humans, but successful in bringing glory to God and people to His saving grace. Waiting *in* Him means making sure we are connected to the source so we don't become weary, just like the trees planted along the riverbank are connected to the water. Stay connected by poring over the Word and allowing His words to soak into your life.

David was so connected to the Lord that he was called a man after God's own heart. As David was running and hiding from Saul, the man who was pursuing him to kill him, he prayed to stay close to the Lord. After David became king, however, he strayed away from the Lord anytime he focused on himself and allowed his own desires to replace the Lord's.

Stay connected to the Lord. SEE His Word bring life, and FEEL the connection between you and Him.

Think About This

What do you need to do to stay connected to Him?

Lord, I long to produce fruit that will be visible to those around me. I long to be so connected to You that anyone who sees me will know that You are the source of my life. Be my life, Lord. May the hope of the gospel run through my veins.

Day 19

Trust in His Strength

But the godly will flourish like palm trees and grow strong like the cedars of Lebanon.

Psalm 92:12

Ezekiel 31 describes the cedars of Lebanon and how they grew strong due to their connection to the deep springs. These trees stood taller than all of the other trees because of their deep connection to their source. They drew their strength from the springs. We can draw on the Lord for our advantage as well. Waiting can seem wearisome at times, but when we call out to Him and stay connected to Him as our source, we find strength and hope.

One of the greatest things that happen when we stay connected to our source, though, is that others will find refuge because of our connection. The birds and other animals took refuge in the beautiful cedars of Lebanon. Likewise, we have a direct impact on how others grow in the Lord.

CALL out His name and BREATHE in His strength and power to help lead you. FEEL His springs of life flow through you.

Think About This

Who do you want to impact, and how, as you wait *in* Him and rely on His strength?

> *Oh Lord, make me like the cedars of Lebanon, connected to You, my source of strength and life. May my life in You flourish and affect everyone around me. I want those close to me to feel the strength and power of Your love. I want those who may come in contact with me to see You shining through me.*

Day 20

TRUST IN HIS GLORY

For all creation is waiting eagerly for that future day when God will reveal who his children really are.

Romans 8:19

Thinking about the future, or even tomorrow, can be challenging during times like these. However, for the Christian, there is a tomorrow, there is a future, and there is an eternity. We *do* have hope we can rely on that fuels our everyday life. We do not wait as one who has no hope. Instead, we actively pursue the Lord *in* our waiting, we read and take hold of His promises, and we delight in our relationship with Him. Every day we focus on this hope instead of our momentary troubles. He is trustworthy and gives us the faith we have for tomorrow. While there may be pain in the waiting, pain in the temporary, and pain in today, we can find joy in life with the Lord.

Turn away from the unfocused things. Turn away from the pain and focus and STRETCH forward to the glory on the other side—a greater anointing, a peaceful heart, the good for those who love the Lord. ENVISION heaven and all of its beauty, and eternal life with the Father.

Think About This

What promises can you take hold of? What pain do you need to turn away from to focus on a future with the Lord?

> *Lord, I know that the troubles we are experiencing during the pandemic are momentary. In the grand scheme of things, they will represent but a small fraction of a more fabulous life with You. So help me refocus on You and the future You have for me. Help me turn away from pain, and hope in Your purpose. You are right, You are trustworthy, and You are eternal.*

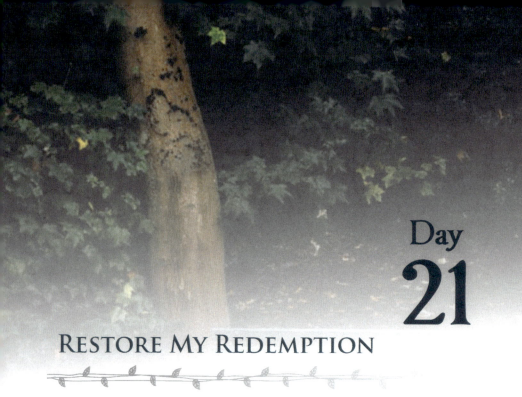

Day 21

RESTORE MY REDEMPTION

O Israel, hope in the Lord;
   For with the Lord, there is unfailing love.
   His redemption overflows.

Psalm 130:7

God is the God of redemption. This is something that most religions don't offer. The chance to start again. The opportunity to wipe the slate clean. Recovery for His people is the whole reason God sent Jesus to earth. He needed to make way for us to be with Him, but sin stood in the way. Sin blocks our view of God and keeps us from being in His presence. So God sent Jesus to be the sacrifice for the dirty, ugly sins in our lives. Jesus bridged the gap between man and God. The word *redeem* means to atone or make amends for. That is precisely what God did: He sent Jesus to be the atonement for our sins and redeem us. So we wait *in* His redemption. Amid our waiting, we delight in how Jesus has made us clean and made way for us.

Child of God, LEAN into Him during this moment of waiting and SHOUT aloud your words of thankfulness. You have been made clean! This act of redemption is a one-time act. Sure, you will still mess up from time to time and need forgiveness, but when Christ redeemed you, He thoroughly cleaned you. Praise Him for that.

Think About This

Have you ever really thanked God for saving and redeeming you? Take time now to spend a few minutes in prayer, thanking Him for what He has done for you.

> *Thank You, Lord, for the beautiful picture of Your redemption. You brought me up out of the pit, rescued me from the darkness, and cleaned my life. Out of Your unfailing love for me, You redeemed my soul. Now nothing is stopping me from living with You forever.*

Day 22

A Full Restoration

On that day the announcement to Jerusalem will be,
  "Cheer up, Zion! Don't be afraid!
*For the L*ORD*, your God is living among you.*
  He is a mighty savior.
He will take delight in you with gladness.
  With his love, he will calm all your fears.
  He will rejoice over you with joyful songs."

Zephaniah 3:16–17

Zephaniah was a prophet who spoke to the Israelites about God's coming judgment. He urged Judah to repent and turn back to the Lord so He would forgive them. The people had no fear of the Lord. Instead, they lived however they wanted and disregarded God and His Word. God would bring wrath upon the people for the way they lived, but then He would bring restoration. These verses promise that once He brought revival to His broken people, He would delight in them, calm their fears, rejoice over them, and live among them. It would be a full restoration.

The word *restore* means to return to a previous condition. It would be as if the people of Israel had never wronged the Lord. Sure, the consequences would remain, but He wiped their sins clean. They would have a fresh start. God wants to restore you, give you a clean start, and live with you. TAKE HOLD of His restoration today and allow Him to be a part of your life.

Think About This

How has God transformed your life? Have you allowed Him to completely restore you?

> *Lord, You restored the Israelites even after they disregarded You and lived for themselves. I live for myself so often, yet You take me back time and time again. I want to live like I've been restored. Help me take hold of Your goodness and what You've done for me.*

Day 23

CLINGING TO HIS WORD

Mary responded,
"Oh, how my soul praises the Lord.
   How my spirit rejoices in God, my Savior!
For he took notice of his lowly servant girl,
   and from now on, all generations will call me blessed.
For the Mighty One is holy,
   and he has done great things for me.
He shows mercy from generation to generation
   to all who fear him.

Luke 1:46–50

Mary, the mother of Jesus, knew that God would carry out His promise to her. She knew she had a purpose that only He could fulfill. The Lord's angel had come and told her that she would be the mother of the Savior. After she went to visit her relative who was also pregnant, Elizabeth told her in verse 45, "You are blessed because you believed that the Lord would do what He said." Mary believed that her Savior would come and deliver her because that's what God had told her He would do. She rejoiced in Him because He saw her. She declared the great things He had done for her. Mary knew what the generations before her and what the prophecies had told her. She had waited for the moment those words would become a reality.

Just like Mary, you can also wait in His Word. His words bring healing. His words can repair broken relationships. His words bring freedom. His words bring restoration to the soul. For Mary, His words brought purpose to her life. READ His Word today and allow them to bring you healing and meaning.

Think About This

What promises have you found in His Word?

> *Lord, You have many promises for me to take hold of. You will fulfill them because You say You will. So I believe that You will do what You say You will do. Give me the faith of Mary. Help me cling to Your words.*

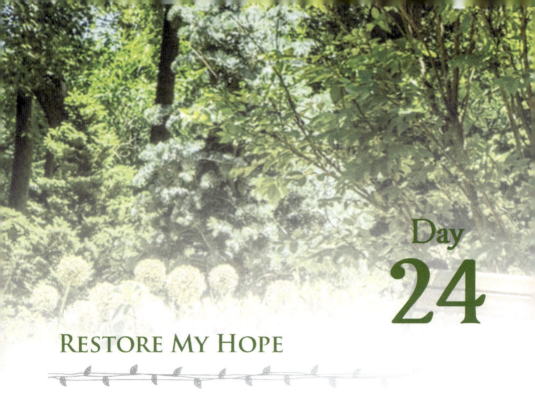

Day 24

RESTORE MY HOPE

> *I wait for the LORD, my soul doth wait, and in His Word do I hope.*
>
> Psalms 130:5 (KJV)

It can be easy to lose hope when times are tough. A grim prognosis, a crumbled relationship, a struggling friendship, a job loss, and many other scenarios threaten to steal our hope. When we place our faith in earthly things, we can lose it fast because those things are temporary. If our hope is in a person and that person disappoints us, as they will, then our hope will vanish.

The person in this verse, though, hopes in God's Word. Hoping in His Word, His promises, and His truth makes waiting seem less difficult—more bearable. His Word is eternal. It never disappoints, and it definitely never disappears. So SIT down with the Lord. WRITE a list of all of the things you can hope in. Close your eyes, dear child, and BREATHE in

His presence. When you hope in His Word, you can find Him *in* the waiting.

Think About This

In what do you place your hope? Are these things temporary or eternal?

> *Lord, in You and Your Word, I hope. I know that You are the only One who will not disappoint me. You promise to be faithful. Lord, help me find myself in the center of Your will so that Your desires become my desires. Then I know I will hope in You.*

Day 25

A Strong Anchor

> *This hope is a reliable and trustworthy anchor for our souls. It leads us through the curtain into God's inner sanctuary.*
>
> Hebrews 6:19

An anchor is a heavy object that hooks to the bottom of the sea and prevents a vessel from moving. It is a small object compared to the vessel it is restricting, so how amazing to think that something so compact serves such a great purpose.

As people, we can anchor ourselves to so many temporary, worthless things. When we anchor ourselves to these, we will find that worldly things provide no strength and are not trustworthy anchors. However, when we anchor ourselves in Christ, He cannot be moved, so our hope and trust in Him won't move either. Our faith only moves when we do not hope in Him. So THINK about what you place your confidence in. STAND in His presence and TELL Him that you are going to anchor yourself to Him!

Your hope is a strong anchor. Your hope is what anchors you to God. If you don't have hope, you'll find your faith wavering. When you place your hope in the living God, you'll be ushered into His inner sanctuary. You will STAND in His presence.

Think About This

What can you do every day to put your faith in Christ as your anchor?

> *Lord, remind me of the strength, revelation, and deeper connection gained when I wait in You. I find strength in You when I place my hope in You like an anchor. God, help me to hope in You every day so that I will find an immovable faith. You are trustworthy. You are strong. Anchor me, O Lord, to You.*

Day 26

RESTORATION IN THE SILENCE

So it is good to wait quietly
 *for salvation from the L*ORD*. ...*
Let them sit alone in silence
 *beneath the L*ORD*'s demands.*
Let them lie face down in the dust,
 for there may be hope at last.

Lamentations 3:26, 28–29

Silence. Silence can be so painful for us to endure. We often have a hard time being silent. We don't like "dead air." We feel the need to speak if no one else is speaking. We feel the need to make our voice known so that we are not just sitting in silence.

The word *lament* means to express sorrow or mourn over. The author of the book of Lamentations was lamenting—expressing deep sorrow for— the destruction of Jerusalem. He describes a sense of regret mixed with grief. Everything had been stripped away from the Israelites. Their only choice now was to sit in silence and wait for the salvation of the Lord. Their shame brought them face down in the dust. It seems like such a bleak picture, but there is always hope during silence. When everything came crashing down, there was still the hope of restoration.

God is a God of restoration. He is the only One who can repair what's been destroyed, restore relationships, and mend the broken. So you do not have to sit in silence as those with no hope. You can delight in knowing that God is with you in the midst of the silence. You can crawl up onto His lap and FEEL His presence as you wait.

Think About This

How can you be silent *in* your waiting but still have hope? READ Lamentations 3 and take comfort in His faithfulness.

> *Lord, I will wait quietly in You, knowing that even when everything is silent, You are still near me. May I feel Your presence wrap around me. May I take comfort in Your words and have hope that You will mend what's been broken.*

Day 27

Wait with Action

*"Be silent before the L*ORD*, all humanity, for he is springing into action from his holy dwelling."*

Zechariah 2:13

Sometimes our waiting can feel like months, even years. It can seem as though God is not working amid His silence. But just because He does not answer when we want Him to answer doesn't mean He is not actively working. In this verse, He is asking us to be silent and trust Him in the waiting. Many times we try to act on our own because we think that God isn't working. He is not only working, he is *springing* into action!

The book of Esther takes place during the four hundred years of silence from God (right before He sent Jesus to earth). Esther, a Hebrew woman and an orphan, lived in a time of Jewish captivity, yet she became queen of the Persian Empire. God had great plans for Esther and the Jews in the midst of captivity. You will not find the name of God in the book of Esther; however, that doesn't mean that God was not at work. He was actively working to rescue Esther and her people from the hands of Haman, an official of King Xerxes, who had the plot to kill the Jews. God delivered the people from His hands and continued to deliver them in the coming years.

God is working even when you cannot see it. You need only to be silent and allow Him to work.

Think About This

Do you tend to let God work or take things into your own hands? Be SILENT today and BASK in His faithfulness. TELL Him that you know He is working all things for your good.

> *Lord, You are so kind and faithful. Help me trust You even when I cannot see what You are doing and how You are working. Your Word says that You are working all things together for my good. I know that You are springing into action. Help me trust in You every day and take comfort in the silence.*

Day 28

WAIT WITH PRAISE

*Be thou exalted, L*ORD*, in thine own strength: so will we sing and praise thy power.*

Psalm 21:13 (KJV)

Waiting *in* Him exposes us to worship, prayer, and a deeper relationship with God in a new way. When we wait *in* Him, we open ourselves up to His praise. The Lord wants us to be still, to listen, and to worship Him. He created us to exalt His name. He created us to worship Him. When we sit back and really see all of what He has done for us, we won't be able to stop praising Him.

Romans 12:1 tells us that offering ourselves as living sacrifices is our spiritual act of worship. So how can you praise and worship Him in the middle of your waiting? Offer your life. Take yourself out of the center. Don't focus on yourself, but on Him and how you can worship Him. When you become Christ-focused instead of self-focused, praise will well up inside you. So before you do anything else today, STAND up, STRETCH your arms to the heavens, and offer praise to your King.

Think About This

What does worship mean to you? How can you worship God every day?

Lord, may the words of my mouth offer up praise and exalt Your name! May the actions of my life demonstrate a life that is sacrificing self and centered around You. May my life be my spiritual act of worship. Help me lift up my life every day. Give me the words when I can't find the words to sing.

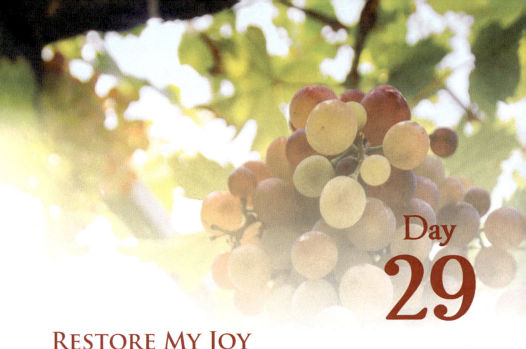

Day 29

Restore My Joy

I will still be joyful and glad
    because the Lord *God is my Savior.*
The sovereign Lord *gives me strength.*
    He makes me sure-footed as a deer
    and keeps me safe on the mountains.

Habakkuk 3:18–19 (GNT)

There is so much to be joyful about. Even while waiting, we can find joy. We can be joyful because the Lord has come to rescue and restore us. We can be glad because He gives us His strength, so we don't have to rely on our own weaknesses. We can take comfort because He makes us sure-footed like a deer. We do not have to worry about stumbling and falling. We can rest in His peace, knowing that He will keep us safe in the mountains. When we allow Him to keep us safe on the mountaintop, we will be safe from our Enemy, the devil. That doesn't mean he won't try to attack us, but we can find ourselves safe in the arms of Christ. He gave us His salvation, and He will protect us from the Enemy.

The joy God gives you is an eternal joy that can never be taken away. You may have a hard time seeing that joy sometimes, because we tend to block our view of His satisfaction with worldly things, but it never leaves. Happiness is a feeling that is temporary and goes away. Joy is everlasting.

Think About This

What spiritual things do you have to be joyful about today? SPEAK them aloud to your Lord. TELL Him what you are thankful for and what brings you joy.

> *Lord, You give me great joy. I know that even when it is difficult for me to see the joy You give, it is still there. Your joy lasts longer than any other feeling or emotion I have. Help me see the joy in every situation. Help me take hold of Your blessing and allow it to consume every part of me.*

Day 30

Restore My Purpose

"For I know the plans I have for you," says the Lord. "They are plans for good and not for disaster, to give you a future and a hope."

Jeremiah 29:11

There is a purpose to everything in this world. Every pain, every sorrow, every trial, every tear, every praise has a purpose. The Lord tells us in Jeremiah that He has plans for His people. These plans are *good* and are not for disaster. His plans are to give His people a future and a hope.

Every minute in the waiting has a purpose. Waiting breaks our rhythm to ourselves. Waiting teaches us how to interact with God. Waiting *in* Him is where we experience the crushing from

    Weeping to walking   Wound to wisdom
    Pain to purpose   Hurt to healing

Rejection to revelation   Pause to passion

Amid the waiting, you will find the Lord actively working out your purpose. You will find Jesus giving salvation and restoring your soul. You will find the Holy Spirit interceding on your behalf. You will find all three claiming your life, working together for your good.

The WAIT is a PAUSE, not a STOP, so God can shift us into His purpose. Waiting *in* Him reveals who we are becoming in the next season. Oh, child of God, wait *in* Him and delight in your purpose today!

Think About This

Do you genuinely BELIEVE He has a purpose for your life? PRAY today, and SPEAK to Him about your purpose.

> *Lord, I know You have a great purpose for my life. You delight in my salvation. You have made a way for me to live with You forever in Your presence. You have given me Jesus, who has offered me salvation and restored my life. You have given me the Holy Spirit, who continually intercedes on my behalf, pleading my case before You and guiding me in the direction I should go. Thank You for waiting with me in the silence and for showing me that I have a purpose.*

Day 31

WAIT WITH PREPARATION

*The horse is prepared for the day of battle,
but victory belongs to the LORD.*

Proverbs 21:31

To take hold of His purpose for our lives, we must ready ourselves and be prepared for the battle during this time of waiting *in* Him. Just as a soldier trains, gathers the equipment he needs, and gets his mind ready for action, so must we also be prepared. We are in the middle of spiritual warfare, so while we are waiting, we need to be preparing for what's to come. The Enemy will attack, and we need to be ready.

Ephesians 6 tells us to put on the armor of God. That's precisely what you need to do while you are waiting *in* Him. Put on the *belt of truth*, so you will know what God says and will be able to LEAN on His promises. Don the *body armor of righteousness;* the Enemy's darts will not penetrate if you are living the right life. Wear the *feet of Good News* and carry the gospel with you everywhere you go. Use the *shield of faith* to block the

Enemy's attacks. Have faith that God is with you. Take up the *helmet of salvation*—trust in His salvation. He has saved you and restored you. Most of all, take the *sword of the Spirit* (His Word) in your hands. READ His Word. STUDY His Word. KNOW His Word.

If you use this time to truly ready yourself for the Enemy's attacks, you will stand firm after the battle is over (see Ephesians 6:14). Why? Victory belongs to the Lord!

Think About This

How can you be prepared for the Enemy's attacks? What do you need to do to be ready while you wait *in* Him?

> *Lord, prepare me by helping me put on the full armor of God! May I take hold of Your salvation and Your truth. Help me be patient in the waiting, confident in Your purpose, and hopeful in Your victory. I want to be a part of what You are doing in the world, so help me be prepared!*

THE END

But he also causes all things to happen at the right time. He puts questions in our minds. We want to know what happens after our death. We cannot understand all the things that God has done. We should enjoy our lives. There is nothing better that we can do than that. We should also do good things during our lives. We should get pleasure from what we eat. We should enjoy what we drink. And we should be happy when we are doing our work. These are all gifts from God. Everything that God does will be for all time. We cannot do anything more than what God has done. We cannot take anything away from what he has done. God wants us to worship him. That is the reason for all that he does. (Ecclesiastes 3:11 Then God said, "You've been going around in circles in these hills long enough; go north. Command the people, You're about to cut through the land belonging to your relatives, the People of Esau who settled in Seir. They are terrified of you, but restrain yourselves. Don't try and start a fight. I am not giving you so much as a square inch of their land. I've already given all the hill country of Seir to Esau—he owns it all. Pay them up front for any food or water you get from them." God, your God, has blessed you in everything you have done. He has guarded you in your travels through this immense wilderness. For forty years now, God, your God, has been right here with you. You haven't lacked one thing. God told me, "And don't try to pick a fight with the Moabites. I am not giving you any of their land. I've given ownership of Ar to the People of Lot." God said, "It's time now to cross the Brook Zered." So we crossed the Brook Zered. (Amos 9:13

"Yes indeed, it won't be long now." God's Decree. "Things are going to happen so fast your head will swim, one thing fast on the heels of the other. You won't be able to keep up. Everything will be happening at once—and everywhere you look, blessings! Blessings like wine pouring off the mountains and hills. I'll make everything right again for my people Israel: "They'll rebuild their ruined cities. They'll plant vineyards and drink good wine. They'll work their gardens and eat fresh vegetables. And I'll plant them, plant them on their own land. They'll never again be uprooted from the land I've given them." God, your God, says so. (Deuteronomy 2:2

Made in the USA
Middletown, DE
12 May 2024

54208073R00044